MOUNT RUSHMORE

Kaite Goldsworthy

www.av2books.com

AV² provides enriched content that supplements and complements this book. Weigl's AV² books strive to create inspired learning and engage young minds in a total learning experience.

Your AV² Media Enhanced books come alive with...

Audio
Listen to sections of the book read aloud.

Key Words
Study vocabulary, and complete a matching word activity.

Video
Watch informative video clips.

Quizzes
Test your knowledge.

Go to www.av2books.com, and enter this book's unique code.

Embedded Weblinks
Gain additional information for research.

Slide Show
View images and captions, and prepare a presentation.

BOOK CODE

T888320

AV² **by Weigl** brings you media enhanced books that support active learning.

Try This!
Complete activities and hands-on experiments.

... and much, much more!

Published by AV² by Weigl
350 5th Avenue, 59th Floor
New York, NY 10118

Website: www.av2books.com   www.weigl.com

Library of Congress Cataloging-in-Publication Data
Goldsworthy, Kaite.
 Mount Rushmore / Kaite Goldsworthy.
    pages cm. -- (Virtual field trip)
 Includes index.
 Summary: "Explores the history, the people, and the science behind the construction of Mount Rushmore. Intended for fourth to sixth grade students"
--Provided by publisher.
 ISBN 978-1-62127-465-0 (hardcover : alk. paper) -- ISBN 978-1-62127-471-1 (softcover : alk. paper)
 1. Mount Rushmore National Memorial (S.D.)--Juvenile literature. I. Title.
 NB237.B6G65 2013
 978.3'93--dc23
                          2012044674

Printed in the United States of America in North Mankato, Minnesota
1 2 3 4 5 6 7 8 9 0 17 16 15 14 13

032013
WEP280213

Editor: Heather Kissock
Design: Terry Paulhus

Every reasonable effort has been made to trace ownership and to obtain permission to reprint copyright material. The publishers would be pleased to have any errors or omissions brought to their attention so that they may be corrected in subsequent printings. Weigl acknowledges Getty Images as its primary image supplier for this title. Page 16B: South Dakota State Historical Society and State Archives

Contents

What Is Mount Rushmore?

Rising above the rolling prairies of South Dakota is a bold sculpture that has been carved into a mountain. Set into the granite wall of Mount Rushmore are the faces of four of the best-known presidents of the United States—George Washington, Thomas Jefferson, Theodore Roosevelt, and Abraham Lincoln. Known as the Mount Rushmore National Memorial, the sculpture attracts almost three million visitors every year.

Mount Rushmore was originally created to bring more tourists to the state. A local historian named Doane Robinson felt that it was important to offer visitors something beyond just scenery. He thought that a **landmark**—an attraction unique to the state—would increase the number of tourists and give them a reason to stay longer.

Robinson's idea quickly gained the support of local politicians, who also wanted to develop the state's tourist industry. They arranged the funding for the project, and the **monument** began to take shape by the late 1920s. Its construction was not an easy task. Building the monument cost the state $989,992.32 and took 14 years to complete.

Mount Rushmore is one of America's most recognizable landmarks.

Snapshot of South Dakota

South Dakota is located in the north-central United States. North Dakota sits on its northern border. Montana and Wyoming lie to the west. South Dakota shares its eastern border with the states of Minnesota and Iowa. The state of Nebraska is located directly south.

INTRODUCING SOUTH DAKOTA

CAPITAL CITY: Pierre

FLAG:

MOTTO: Under God the People Rule

NICKNAME: The Mount Rushmore State

POPULATION: 814,180 (2010)

ADMITTED TO THE UNION: November 2, 1889

CLIMATE: Continental climate with four seasons. Summers are hot, and winters can be very cold.

SUMMER TEMPERATURE: Average temperature of 89° Fahrenheit (32° Celsius)

WINTER TEMPERATURE: Average temperature of 10°F (-12°C)

TIME ZONE: Central Standard Time (CST) and Mountain Standard Time (MST)

North Dakota

South Dakota

Pierre ★

Nebraska

South Dakota

★ State Capital   ⌐⌐ State Boundary

N

0   250 miles

0   250 kilometers

South Dakota Symbols

South Dakota has several official symbols. Some symbols represent the features that distinguish the area from other parts of the United States. Others indicate the unique place South Dakota has in the history of the country.

OFFICIAL FLOWER
American Pasqueflower

OFFICIAL BIRD
Ring-necked Pheasant

OFFICIAL TREE
Black Hills Spruce

A Step Back in Time

When Robinson first developed the idea of the mountain sculpture, he wanted it to feature figures that represented the American West. He envisioned a mountain with the faces of western icons. Wild West showman Buffalo Bill Cody and explorers Lewis and Clark were just some of the people he thought should be in the sculpture.

To bring his vision to reality, Robinson hired a skilled sculptor named Gutzon Borglum. Borglum had been working on another mountain sculpture in Georgia called the **Confederate** Memorial Carving.

CONSTRUCTION TIMELINE

1923
On December 28, South Dakota State Historian Doane Robinson suggests that a mountain carving be made to create a tourist attraction for South Dakota.

1925
A bill is passed on March 5 to allow the carving of a mountain in Custer State Park.

1927
President Calvin Coolidge dedicates the site on August 10.

1927
Drilling begins on October 4.

1930
The sculpture of George Washington's head is completed and dedicated on July 4.

Calvin Coolidge was the 30th president of the United States. He held the office from 1923 to 1929.

George Washington was supposed to be placed in the middle of the sculpture. Plans changed when the rock to Washington's right was to be too weak for carving.

Borglum liked the idea of creating a tourist attraction for South Dakota, but felt that the American West theme might limit the number of visitors. He believed that the sculpture should be a monument to all of the country. This would allow it to appeal to a broader audience. Borglum felt that people from all parts of the United States would come to see a carving of past presidents. Robinson agreed, and Borglum began work on the sculpture.

Although the creation of Mount Rushmore spanned 14 years, it is estimated that only 6.5 years were spent actually working on it.

1936
Thomas Jefferson's head is completed and dedicated on August 30.

1937
Abraham Lincoln's head is completed and dedicated on September 17.

1939
Theodore Roosevelt's sculpture is finished and dedicated on July 2.

1941
Gutzon Borglum dies. His son, Lincoln, continues his father's work on the sculpture.

1941
Work on Mount Rushmore ends on October 31. The sculpture is considered completed.

Originally, the monument was to feature only two presidents—Washington and Lincoln. Borglum felt that these two presidents would attract more national interest.

Workers on the mountain included miners, sculptors, and rock climbers.

Mount Rushmore's Location

Mount Rushmore is found in the Black Hills of South Dakota. This mountain range extends from the state's Great Plains region into the neighboring state of Wyoming. The range is 125 miles (201 kilometers) long and 65 miles (105 km) wide. The Black Hills are made of a type of rock called granite.

The Black Hills have many interesting types of rock formations. Doane Robinson originally wanted the monument to be carved in a part of the Black Hills called the Needles. The Needles are tall towers or pillars of granite rock that have been naturally **eroded** over time. Gutzon Borglum felt that the Needles were too thin to support carving or sculpting. He chose Mount Rushmore, near Keystone, South Dakota, for the site. The granite was better quality, and it was the tallest peak in the area. It also faced southeast and would receive good light.

Mount Rushmore was named after Charles Rushmore, a New York lawyer who came to the area to check on mining opportunities.

Mount Rushmore Today

Mount Rushmore stands high in the Black Hills as a symbol of the United States. Although weather has created small **hairline** cracks over time, the monument looks almost the same as it did when completed in 1941.

Faces Each eye is 11 feet (3.4 meters) wide. Each mouth is approximately 18 feet (5.5 m) across. All the noses are 20 feet (6 m) long, except that of George Washington, which is 21 feet (6.4 m) in length.

Elevation Mount Rushmore is 5,725 feet (1,745 m) tall.

500 feet (152.4 m)

400 feet (121.9 m)

Height The entire monument is 500 feet (152.4 m) high and 400 feet (121.9 m) wide. The faces are each approximately 60 feet (18.3 m) tall. This is about as tall as a six-story building.

The Structure of Mount Rushmore

Gutzon Borglum wanted Mount Rushmore to be a tribute to the United States. He chose to sculpt Presidents Washington, Jefferson, Roosevelt, and Lincoln because he felt they best represented the country's history. Borglum saw Mount Rushmore as a place for U.S. citizens to understand and honor their past.

George Washington George Washington's sculpture is located on the far left of Mount Rushmore. Washington was the first president of the United States and is known as one of the nation's **founding fathers**. Before becoming president, Washington played a key role in the Revolutionary War, doing much to help the United States gain independence from Great Britain.

In recognition of his importance to the United States, Washington's head is the most prominent on Mount Rushmore.

Thomas Jefferson is also known as the person who wrote the U.S. Declaration of Independence.

Thomas Jefferson Thomas Jefferson's sculpture is located next to that of Washington. Jefferson served as the United States' third president, from 1801 until 1809. Jefferson was responsible for negotiating the **Louisiana Purchase** from France in 1803. The purchase almost doubled the size of the United States at the time.

Theodore Roosevelt Theodore Roosevelt's sculpture is located between the faces of Thomas Jefferson and Abraham Lincoln. As the 26th president of the United States, Theodore Roosevelt served two terms, from 1901 until 1909. His leadership came at a time of great growth in the United States. While many large businesses were thriving and gaining power, Roosevelt worked to ensure the rights of the country's working class.

Theodore Roosevelt was 42 when be became president of the United States. He is the youngest president the country has ever had.

The Hall of Records is only accessible via a very steep trail. It is closed to the public due to safety concerns.

Hall of Records Gutzon Borglum's original plans included a Hall of Records. It was to hold all of the nation's important documents and tell its story as a country. Although it was begun, the Hall of Records was never completed because of cost. In 1998, 16 tablets with copies of important documents such as the Declaration of Independence, the Constitution, and the Bill of Rights were sealed in a wooden box and placed in a **vault** in the unfinished Hall of Records. The entrance was sealed with a giant 1,200-pound (544-kilogram) stone.

Abraham Lincoln On the far right side of Mount Rushmore is the face of Abraham Lincoln. As the 16th president of the United States, Abraham Lincoln served from 1861 until his death in 1865. Lincoln was president during the Civil War and worked to unite a divided country. Lincoln is well-known for his work to abolish slavery.

Abraham Lincoln served in the Illinois legislature and worked as a lawyer prior to becoming president.

VIRTUAL TOUR

Mount Rushmore National Memorial is open every day except Christmas Day. Hours are 8:00 a.m. to 10:00 p.m. in the summer and 8:00 a.m. until 5:00 p.m. in the winter.

Features of Mount Rushmore

Although the presidents' faces are the main attraction, there are many other areas of interest at Mount Rushmore National Monument. Viewing areas and trails have been added to the grounds. This allows visitors the chance to view the monument from different angles.

Visitor and Information Centers

The Information Center is the first building visitors enter when they arrive at Mount Rushmore. Park rangers are there to give maps, information, and tours. The Lincoln Borglum Visitor Center is where visitors go to learn more about the monument. It features films about the carving of Mount Rushmore and many historic photographs.

The visitor center is named after Gutzon Borglum's son, who worked on Mount Rushmore with his father.

The Avenue of Flags directs visitors toward Mount Rushmore.

Avenue of Flags The Avenue of Flags was added to the site in 1976 for the United States **Bicentennial**. It is a walkway lined with 56 flags. Each flag represents a state, district, or territory of the United States. The flags are placed alphabetically, and each flagpole shows the date of statehood.

Viewing Terraces Mount Rushmore has two viewing areas. The Grand View Terrace passes through the Avenue of Flags. This terrace provides some of the best views of Mount Rushmore. A path on the right side of the Grand View Terrace leads to the Borglum Viewing Terrace. A different view of Mount Rushmore can be seen from here.

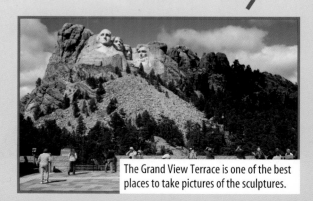

The Grand View Terrace is one of the best places to take pictures of the sculptures.

Lakota, Nakota, and Dakota Heritage Village In the summer, just off the Presidential Trail, three **tipis** can be found at the Lakota, Nakota, and Dakota Heritage Village. Educators from South Dakota's American Indian groups teach visitors about their traditions and culture and the effect the arrival of European settlers had on them.

The Lakota, Nakota, and Dakota Heritage Village allows visitors to learn about the traditions and stories of local American Indian communities.

Along the Presidential Trail are viewpoints and facts about each president on Mount Rushmore.

Presidential Trail The Presidential Trail is a half-mile (0.8-km) walking trail. It allows visitors to get much closer to the mountain. It begins at Grand View Terrace and loops back. More than 400 wooden stairs allow visitors to climb part way up the mountain and down toward the Sculptor's Studio.

Sculptor's Studio The Sculptor's Studio, where Gutzon Borglum worked, is open to visitors in the summer months. Inside the studio are many of the working models and tools used in the creation of the monument. Photographs show Mount Rushmore before, during, and after it was carved.

Plaster models inside the studio show that Borglum originally planned to sculpt the presidents from the waist up.

Big Ideas behind Mount Rushmore

Much planning was needed before the sculpting of Mount Rushmore could begin. Gutzon Borglum had to find a site that would support the sculpture. He also had to develop methods to make sure that his design plans transferred properly to the rock face. Borglum relied on science to make sure his project was a success.

Borglum played a key role in creating the models, siting the sculpture, and planning the work flow. He left the daily supervision of the site to his assistants, including his son Lincoln.

Ratios

When Gutzon Borglum first began designing the sculpture, he worked with models. Borglum spent hours studying photographs, paintings, and even life masks of the presidents so he could create detailed **plaster** models to work from. The models were 1:12 ratio, meaning that every inch (2.5 centimeters) on the model was equal to one foot (30 cm) on Mount Rushmore. He created a "pointing machine" that measured the distance of specific points on the model in relation to other points. These points were then multiplied by 12 and marked on the mountain. He used these marks as guides when the actual sculpting began.

Sculpting with Dynamite

Granite is a very hard rock to sculpt by traditional methods. Using only hammers and chisels on a project the size of Mount Rushmore would have taken too much time. Borglum decided to use dynamite to speed up the process. He used dynamite to remove large amounts of rock so that detailed chiseling and carving could be done. The basic head shapes were blasted out first. Then, workers were suspended in special seats called bosun chairs so they could use drills, chisels, and hammers to create the details of the faces.

Approximately 90 percent of the sculpting of Mount Rushmore was done by dynamite.

Science at Work at Mount Rushmore

Mount Rushmore was sculpted using a variety of tools. Power tools were used for much of the work, but simple machines helped give the sculpture detail. Simple machines are tools that use scientific principles to make work easier.

Drills

Workers used **pneumatic** drills to shape the faces on Mount Rushmore. Pneumatic drills are powered by **pressurized** air. The air is held in a tank called a compressor. The compressor pressurizes the air and sends it through a thick hose that is connected to the drill. A pneumatic drill has a metal casing with a long drill **bit** attached. Inside the casing are tubes, a valve, and a solid metal rod called a pile driver. When air is forced through the tubes by the compressor, the pile driver is pushed down onto the bit. This moves the bit down, causing it to strike the work surface. The downward movement of the drill bit turns the valve inside the casing over, changing the direction of the air. This change of direction pushes the drill back up and away from the work surface.

A pneumatic drill can strike a surface an average of 1,500 times per minute.

Chisels

To chip away at the smaller pieces of rock, workers used chisels. A chisel is a type of simple machine called a wedge. Wedges are wider at one end than at the other. They are used to push things apart. When the narrow part of a wedge is inserted between two objects, it begins to separate them. It does this by converting force on one end into a splitting motion at the other end. The splitting occurs at right angles to the pointed part of the wedge. Wedges can also be used to lift objects and to hold them in place.

Chisels can be used to cut and shape stone, wood, or metal.

VIRTUAL TOUR

During Mount Rushmore's construction, more than 450,000 tons (408,233 tonnes) of granite rock were removed from the mountain.

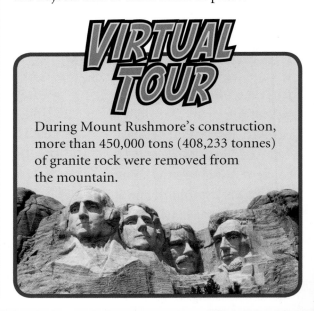

Mount Rushmore's Builders

Gutzon Borglum was the only artist at the time with experience carving mountains. He brought his knowledge of mountain carving to Mount Rushmore. More than 400 workers worked on Mount Rushmore. Even though there were risks, no workers lost their lives.

Gutzon Borglum was already 60 years old when he began work on Mount Rushmore.

Gutzon Borglum Sculptor

Gutzon Borglum was born in 1867, in Idaho to Danish immigrants. Borglum studied art as a young man. While studying in Paris, he met French sculptor Auguste Rodin, who is famous for sculptures such as *The Thinker* and *The Kiss*. Rodin became a source of inspiration for Borglum. When Borglum returned to the United States, he began to focus on sculpting. A **bust** he made of Abraham Lincoln was displayed at the White House while Theodore Roosevelt was president. Borglum was known for being very stubborn and a **perfectionist**. Many people found him brilliant but difficult to work with. He died before seeing his greatest work, Mount Rushmore, finished.

Lincoln Borglum
Sculptor

Lincoln Borglum was born in 1912, to Gutzon Borglum and his second wife, Mary. Lincoln was named for his father's favorite president, Abraham Lincoln. Lincoln was just a young man when his father began working on Mount Rushmore. He was there the day the site was chosen and for every dedication. Lincoln started working on Mount Rushmore when he was 21. He was talented like his father. Over time, Lincoln became **superintendent** of the project. He was responsible for finishing it after his father died.

Lincoln Borglum sculpted a bust of his father. It now sits outside Mount Rushmore's visitor center.

Doane Robinson Historian

Doane Robinson was born in 1856, in Wisconsin. He was originally a farmer but studied to become a lawyer. He also had a love of history. This led Robinson to become South Dakota's State Historian. Although it is often forgotten, it was Robinson's idea to create a memorable attraction in the Black Hills. For this reason, he is often called the Father of Mount Rushmore. Robinson worked very hard to pass laws and raise money to allow Mount Rushmore National Memorial to be built.

Doane Robinson died in 1946, at the age of 90, but he lived to see his dream become a reality.

Sculptors

Sculptors are artists who create works of art that are **three-dimensional**. They use many different materials, including stone, marble, metal, wood, glass, clay, and paper. A sculptor can create a sculpture by adding and shaping material, or by carving and taking away material. Sculptors use different tools, depending on the material they are working with. Hammers and chisels, for instance, are used for stone carving. When working with clay, sculptors often use only their hands.

Sculptors can create a variety of artworks, ranging from realistic to abstract. Many sculptors specialize in the human form.

Blasters

Blasters are also known as explosives engineers. They know the safest and most effective way to use explosives to remove rock for construction projects. Blasters can also work in the mining and metals industries. An explosives engineer has to know how to use the many different types of explosives. They also must know about the type of rock or other material they are blasting.

Explosives engineers are responsible for selecting the proper explosives and taking the appropriate measures to control the blast.

Stone Carvers

A stone carver is an artist or craftsman who works only in stone. Stone carvers know about the qualities found in different varieties of stone, such as hardness or softness. They know which tools to use and how to work with each type. Stone carvers use traditional tools such as chisels, hammers, and mallets as well as modern power and pneumatic tools.

Stone carvings start as a piece of natural stone. Carvers chip and shave away pieces of the stone to give the carving its shape.

Similar Structures around the World

Mount Rushmore is just one of many sculptures that have been carved into mountains. Around the world and throughout time, people have spent many years creating monuments that would last.

Crazy Horse Memorial

BUILT: 1948–present
LOCATION: Black Hills, South Dakota, United States
DESIGN: Korczak Ziolkowski and Henry Standing Bear
DESCRIPTION: The Crazy Horse Memorial will be the world's largest mountain sculpture when it is finally completed. It shows Lakota leader Crazy Horse riding a horse and pointing into the distance. The purpose of the memorial is to preserve and celebrate the heritage, traditions, and culture of North American Indians.

The Confederate Memorial Carving is spread across 130,680 square feet (12,141 sq. m) of Stone Mountain.

Confederate Memorial Carving

BUILT: 1914–1972
LOCATION: DeKalb County, Georgia, United States
DESIGN: Gutzon Borglum, Augustus Lukeman, Walker Kirkland Hancock
DESCRIPTION: The Confederate Memorial Carving is the world's highest **relief** sculpture. It is 400 feet (122 m) above the base of Stone Mountain. The memorial honors three Confederate heroes of the U.S. Civil War—Jefferson Davis, General Lee, and General "Stonewall" Jackson.

Crazy Horse's head alone is 87.5 feet (26.5 m) high. The final sculpture is expected to be more than 600 feet (183 m) wide.

Temple of Ramses II

BUILT: 1269–1256 BC
LOCATION: Abu Simbel, Egypt
DESIGN: Unknown
DESCRIPTION: King Ramses II ruled Egypt from 1279 to 1213 BC. During that time, he built several structures along the Nile River. The Temple of Ramses was one of these structures. It was built to honor the gods Ptah, Amun-Re, and Re-Harakhte. The entrance to the Temple of Ramses is guarded by four seated statues of Ramses II that have been carved out of the limestone cliffs. Each figure is about 65 feet (20 m) tall.

The Temple of Ramses II was buried under sand for many years. It was rediscovered in 1813.

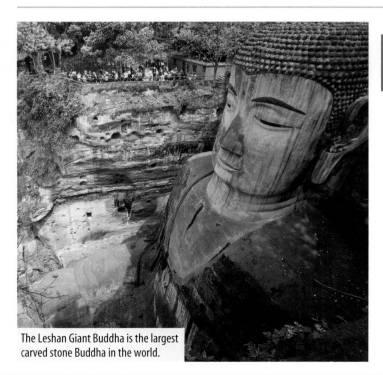

The Leshan Giant Buddha is the largest carved stone Buddha in the world.

Leshan Giant Buddha

BUILT: 713–803 AD
LOCATION: Leshan City, China
DESIGN: Monk Hai Tong
DESCRIPTION: China's Leshan Giant Buddha was built at the point where three rivers meet. It was hoped that the presence of the Buddha would calm the rough waters found there. Carved into a mountainside, the statue of the seated Buddha is 233 feet (71 m) high and 92 feet (28 m) wide.

Issues Facing Mount Rushmore

Mount Rushmore has become the symbol of U.S. history that Gutzon Borglum intended. People come from all over the world to see it. However, the sculpture is facing both political and environmental issues that need to be addressed so that future generations can experience and understand its importance.

WHAT IS THE ISSUE?

Although it is estimated that Mount Rushmore only loses 1 inch (2.5 cm) of stone every 10,000 years, erosion due to weather is still a threat to the monument.

The Black Hills of South Dakota are considered sacred to the Sioux tribes. An 1868 **treaty** gave the Black Hills to the Sioux people, but a law in 1877 took the land away.

EFFECTS

Weathering breaks down the granite, and water freezing in the cracks causes pieces of the rock to break off over time.

Many American Indian groups were upset when Mount Rushmore was created. They protested the loss of land, claiming that it had alienated them from their heritage and from the rest of the country.

ACTION TAKEN

Experts take special photos of the monument from a helicopter and an airplane. They use these photos to help them locate cracks or places where future cracks may begin. Any cracks can then be filled with silicone.

The U.S. Supreme Court awarded money to the Sioux for this land claim in 1980, but the Sioux did not accept the settlement. In 2012, the United Nations recommended the land, including Mount Rushmore, be returned to the Sioux. No action has been taken so far.

Draw a Picture Using Ratios

A ratio shows the value or size of two different things in relation to each other. For example, if a class of 25 students had 11 boys and 14 girls, it would have a ratio of 11:14. When using ratios in art, a grid is placed over the image that is to be enlarged. If the artist wants to enlarge the image five times, a grid that is five times bigger is drawn out and the image transferred a box at a time. This activity shows how grids work to make a large copy of a smaller image.

Materials
- 1 sheet of white paper
- pencil
- eraser
- ruler
- an image of a single item to be enlarged

Instructions

1. Using the ruler and pencil, measure your image. Mark 1 inch (2.5 cm) sections along each edge. Use your ruler to line up your 1 inch (2.5 cm) marks, then draw vertical and horizontal lines across the picture. This will create a grid of 1 inch (2.5 cm) squares.

2. Take the sheet of paper you will be transferring the image to. You will be working with a 1:2 ratio, so the paper will need to be double the size of your original image.

3. Using your ruler, divide your paper into 2-inch (5-cm) squares. You will have the same number of squares as on your image. However, each square will be double the size. Draw the grid lightly, as you will be erasing the grid lines when you are finished.

4. Look at your original image. Starting at the square in the top left corner, draw what you see in that square on the matching larger square on your paper. When you have finished that square, move to the next and so on until the image is complete.

5. Carefully erase the grid lines. Is your drawing a larger version of the original image?

Mount Rushmore Quiz

Q Why was Mount Rushmore sculpted?

A To bring more tourists to South Dakota

Q How many tons of granite were removed during carving?

A 450,000 tons (408,233 tonnes)

Q How tall is each president's face?

A 60 feet (18.3 m) tall

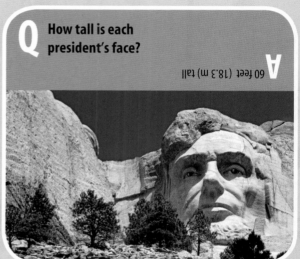

Q What is the name of the trail that leads visitors below the faces?

A The Presidential Trail

Glossary

bicentennial: the 200th anniversary of an event

bit: the cutting part of a drill

bust: a sculpture of a person's head and shoulders

Confederate: representing a republic formed in 1861, composed of the 11 Southern states that seceded from the United States in order to preserve slavery and states' rights

eroded: worn away due to water, ice, or wind

founding fathers: the men who wrote the U.S. Constitution

hairline: a very fine line

landmark: an object or feature of the land that is easily recognizable

Louisiana Purchase: territory sold by France to the United States, extending from the Mississippi River to the Rocky Mountains between the Gulf of Mexico and the Canadian border

monument: a statue or building that is built to honor or pay tribute to a person or event

perfectionist: a person who wants things to be perfect

plaster: a building material made of lime, sand, or cement and water, that dries hard

pneumatic: operated by air or other gases under pressure

pressurized: put under a greater than normal pressure

relief: the projection of figures or forms from a flat background

superintendent: a person who manages an activity or job

three-dimensional: an object that has height, width, and depth and is not flat

tipis: cone-shaped tents traditionally made from wooden poles and animal skins

treaty: a formal agreement between two countries or states

vault: a large room or area for storage

weathering: the breaking down of rocks and other materials by the action of wind, rain, and other elements

Index

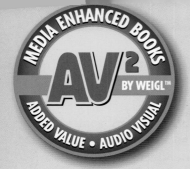

Log on to www.av2books.com

AV² by Weigl brings you media enhanced books that support active learning. Go to www.av2books.com, and enter the special code found on page 2 of this book. You will gain access to enriched and enhanced content that supplements and complements this book. Content includes video, audio, weblinks, quizzes, a slide show, and activities.

AV² Online Navigation

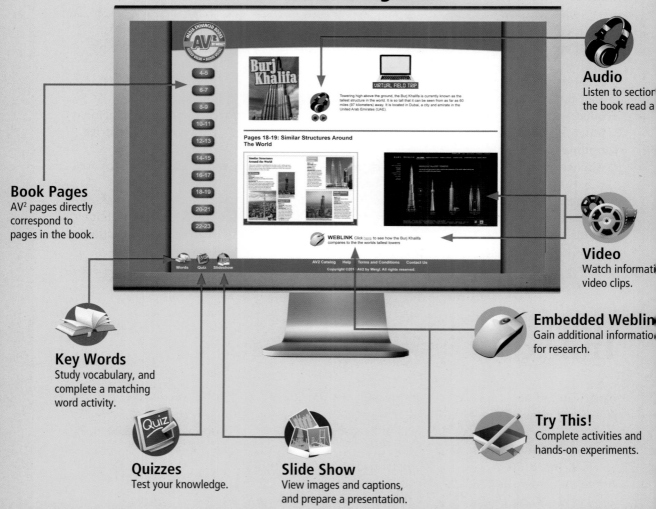

Book Pages
AV² pages directly correspond to pages in the book.

Key Words
Study vocabulary, and complete a matching word activity.

Quizzes
Test your knowledge.

Slide Show
View images and captions, and prepare a presentation.

Audio
Listen to section the book read a

Video
Watch informati video clips.

Embedded Weblin
Gain additional informatio for research.

Try This!
Complete activities and hands-on experiments.

AV² was built to bridge the gap between print and digital. We encourage you to tell us what you like and what you want to see in the future.

Sign up to be an AV² Ambassador at www.av2books.com/ambassador.